Wanderlust

Edna St. Vincent Millay
(1892–1950)

MARIANNE FORMAN

Gently, with imagination ♩ = 120

SAND BLOCKS*

TRIANGLE
TRAIN WHISTLE

SOPRANO
ALTO

My

TENOR
BASS

PIANO

mp

mp

heart is warm with the friends I make, and

S.
A.

T.
B.

---

* The part for sand blocks may be substituted by singers rubbing their palms together.

Duration: 4 mins

Printed in Great Britain

OXFORD UNIVERSITY PRESS, MUSIC DEPARTMENT, GREAT CLARENDON STREET, OXFORD OX2 6DP

4

The rail - road track___ is miles a - way,___ and the day is loud___ with voic - es speak-ing,___

hear   its en-gine   steam-ing.

hear   its   en-gine   steam-ing.

Tempo I ♩ = 120

Tempo I ♩ = 120

dim.

tsh   tsh__   tsh   tsh__   tsh   tsh__   tsh   tsh__

dim.

Tempo I ♩ = 120

dim.

* Singers may optionally put their arms around each other's shoulders until measure 75.

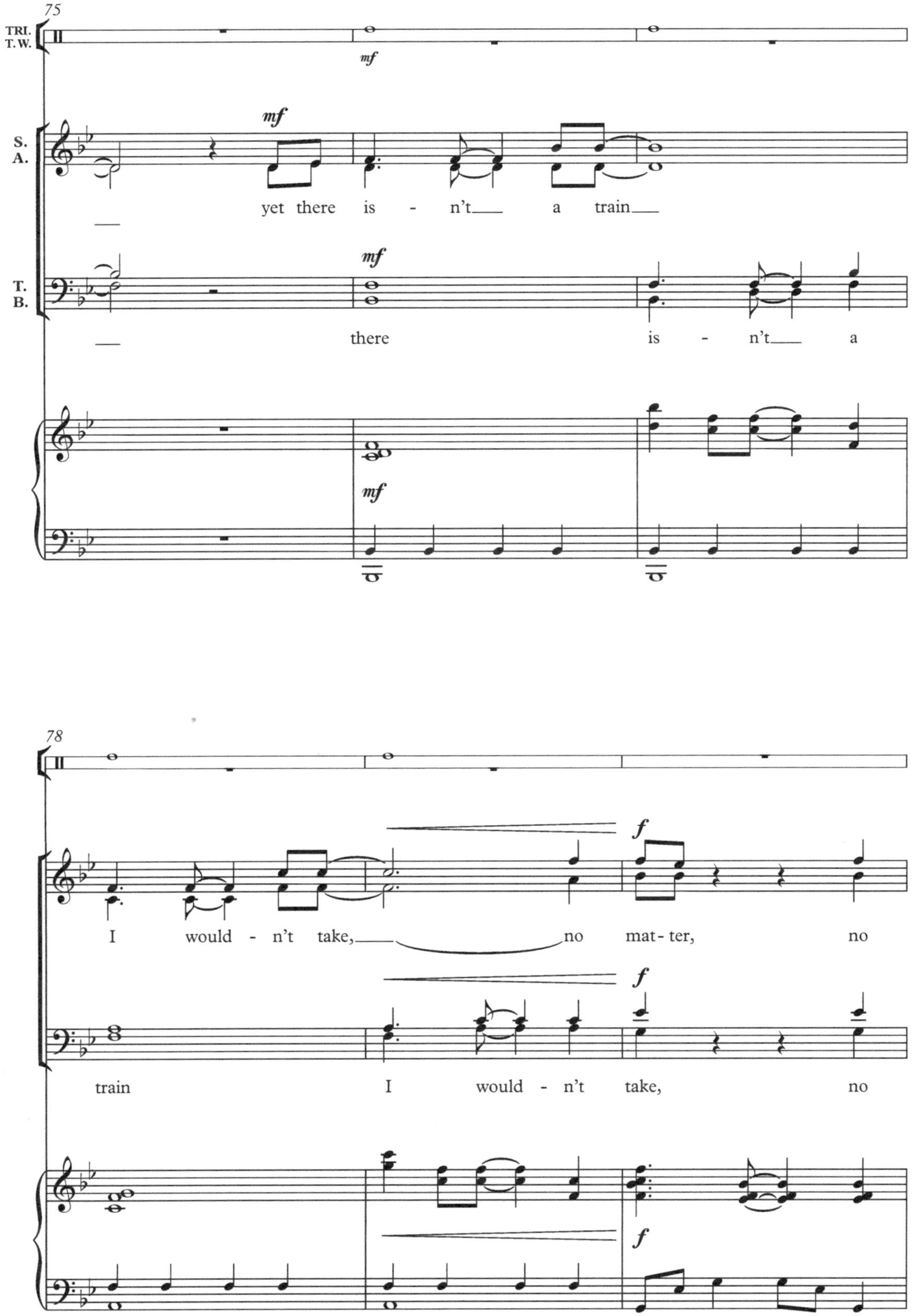
75
TRI.
T.W.
S.
A.
mf
yet there is - n't a train
T.
B.
there is - n't a
78
f
I would - n't take, no mat- ter, no
train I would - n't take, no

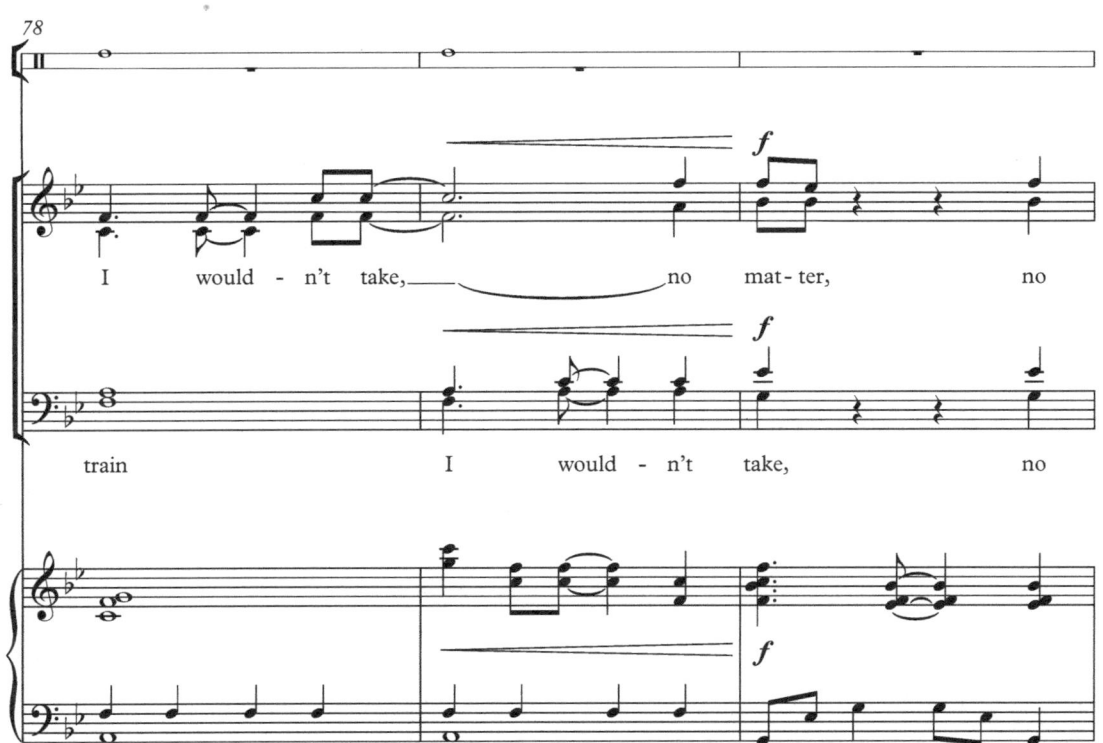

Wanderlust

Edna St. Vincent Millay
(1892–1950)

MARIANNE FORMAN

* The part for sand blocks may be substituted by singers rubbing their palms together.

This part may be enlarged on a photocopier to facilitate performance.

© Oxford University Press 2024 and 2025

43
rit.
dim.
49
Slower ♩ = 60
accel.
6
4
f
60
Tempo I ♩ = 120
senza rit.
f
f
65
11
9
rit.
mf
90
a tempo
p
ff
95
rit.
p

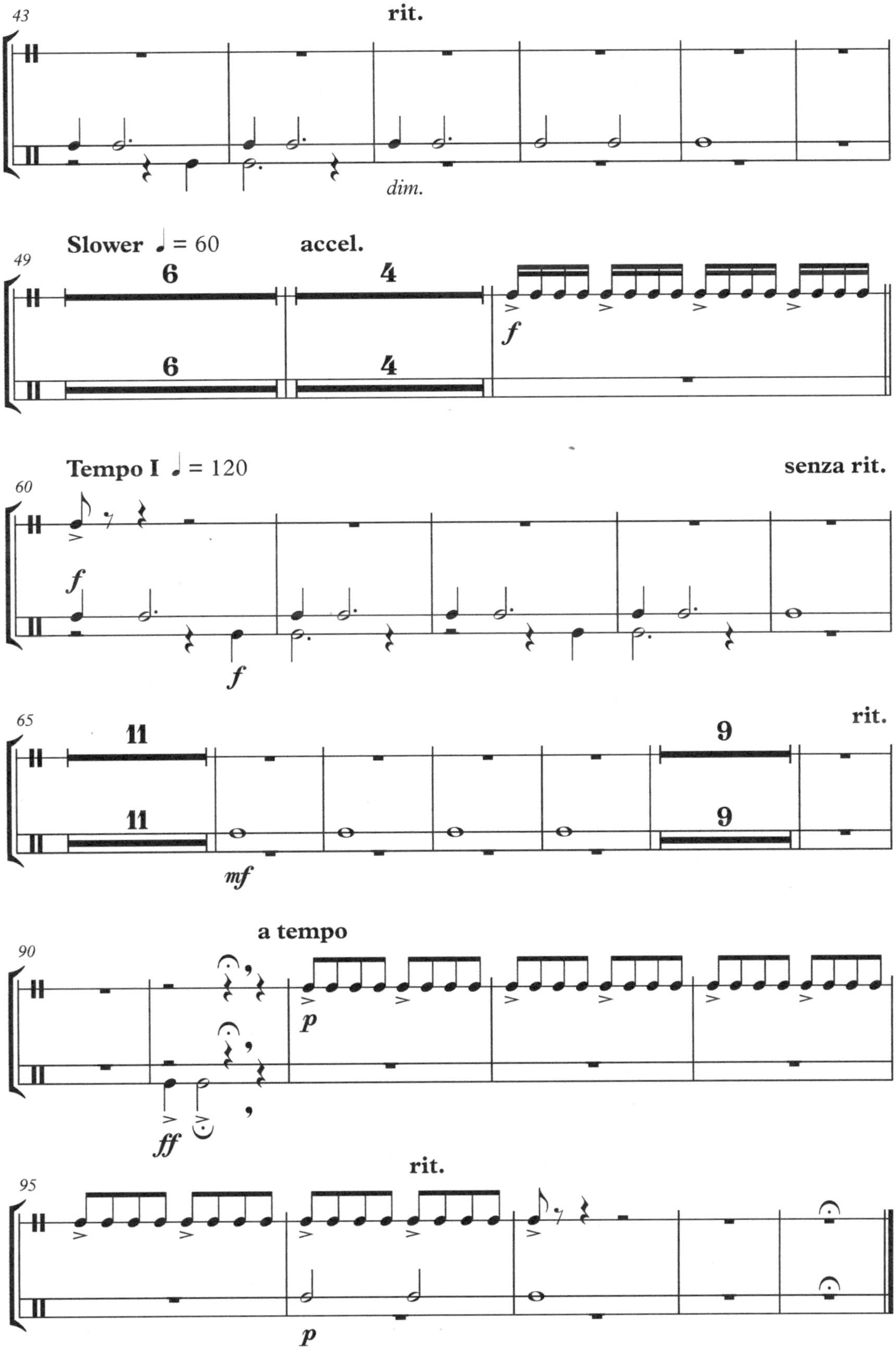

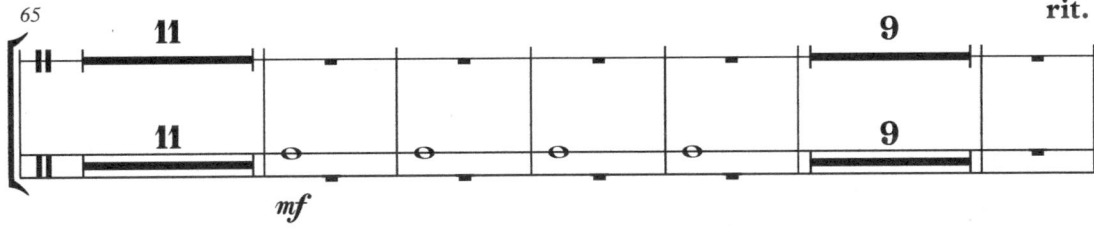

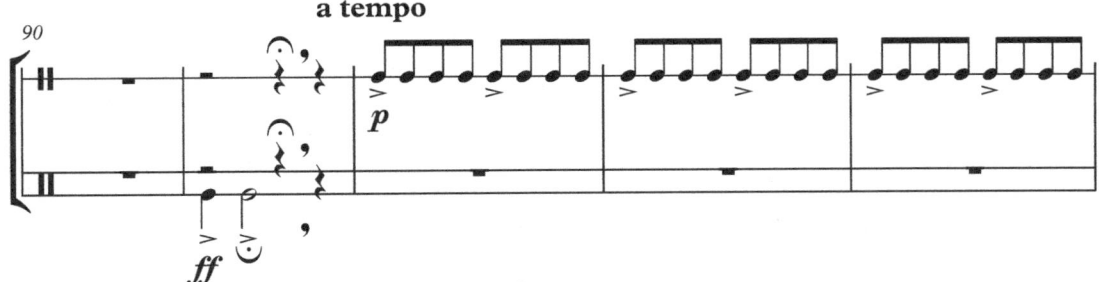

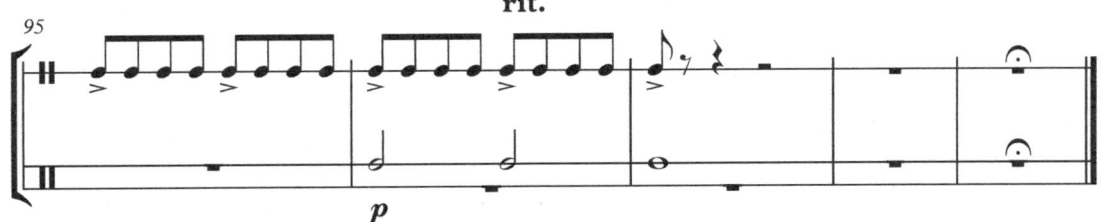

voiceJunction

Voice Junction is an inspirational concert series for all modern mixed-voice singing groups. A meeting point of various styles, the series is fresh, popular, and alternative in feel, and includes new original works—both accompanied and *a cappella*—alongside unique arrangements of well-known tunes. Whether performed by a one-per-part vocal group or a community choir, this is music that brings people together.

Marianne Forman has been arranging and composing music since childhood, and she remains passionate about creating music that is both beautiful and functional. A four-time attendee of the John Ness Beck Foundation Composers' Workshop and recipient of an honourable mention in the King's Singers New Music Prize, she won both categories of the Stockton Chorale Emerging Women Composers Competition in 2023. Her sacred and concert choral pieces have been performed around the world and are appreciated for their compelling melodies and accessible settings. In addition to composing, Marianne is an adjudicator and private piano tutor in San Diego, California.

www.oup.com

ISBN 978-0-19-357936-1

9 780193 579361

OXFORD